T0010416

THE VIEUX CARRÉ

THE VIEUX CARRÉ

JOHN DeMERS

LOUISIANA STATE UNIVERSITY PRESS
BATON ROUGE

Published by Louisiana State University Press
lsupress.org

Manufactured in the United States of America
First printing

Designer: Mandy McDonald Scallan
Typeface: Arno Pro
Printer and binder: Integrated Book International (IBI)

The frontispiece photo is reproduced courtesy of the Hotel Monteleone.

Cover photograph courtesy Sam Gregory Anselmo.

Cataloging-in-Publication Data are available from the Library of Congress.
ISBN 978-0-8071-7855-3 (cloth: alk. paper)

To Muriel, my favorite cocktail partner. Cheers!

CONTENTS

CHAPTER ONE

An Invention You Can Pour

Robert Fulton, Eli Whitney, Thomas Edison, Alexander Graham Bell, Guglielmo Marconi—all names of great inventors who changed the way we live for a time or forever. But not every gifted inventor's name is known to us, and, even around the New Orleans French Quarter, you'd have to skim for a while to come across the name Walter Bergeron. Bergeron was a bartender, you see. A man who fixed cocktails for customers in the bar of a legendary New Orleans hotel. His invention is a thing that's consumed—

1

and typically good to the last drop. At the time of its creation in the 1930s, during the middle of the Great Depression and shortly before World War II made the globe whole lot smaller, Bergeron would name his cocktail after the traditional French section of the town where he lived. And he would strive to include in his invention five products from five different parts of the world that contributed to making his city unique.

For the most part, we don't memorialize bartenders as inventors, but perhaps we should. Whether it's a new recipe for a cocktail or a welcoming smile on a chilly, rainy night, or maybe a piece of an overheard anecdote that cheers us, bartenders *are* inventors. Yet because their inventions are consumed, we don't necessarily remember the names of their creators, much less write them down for posterity. Each time we hear the name Walter Bergeron around the neighborhood the French settlers took to calling Vieux Carré (Old Square), we realize again that the drink he crafted at the Hotel Monteleone is actually a big deal. The Sazerac may have been the earliest local cocktail to gain a following, and the Ramos Gin Fizz may have accumulated the most political clout, both in Louisiana and later Washington, D.C.—but only the Vieux Carré cocktail is able to subtitle its calling card: The Flavors That Made New Orleans.

"Walter Bergeron is kind of one of those guys who fell off the face of the earth when he died," offers Marvin Allen, a bartender at the hotel's Carousel Bar and quasi-official "historian" of the place, a role he defines as a "nerd who likes doing research." "Nobody knows a whole lot about him. He came up with the drink in the early thirties, when he was head bartender in the Lobby Bar, which the hotel had before Mr. Monteleone decided the Carousel Bar would be fun after World War II. Walter had passed away by then. But the Vieux Carré cocktail lived on."

Still, if its admirers assume the Vieux Carré was sipped or slugged in the Carousel since Day One and through all three of the hotel's extensive renovations, they are wrong. The drink was in some ways both behind and ahead of its time, subject of course to the not-always-impressive whims of America's taste in cocktails. Created after Prohibition, it missed out on being part of the cocktail craze that made other libations famous. The years before Prohibition, you'll hear time and again, were America's Cocktail Golden Age. Yet because it closely resembles the booze-forward flavors (and wallop) of the Sazerac and other earlier drinks, the Vieux Carré had to wait for its "carousel" (yes, the pun was intended, unfortunately) to come back around. This didn't happen until the next cocktail craze as late as the 1980s.

The information we do have about the cocktail—indeed what Marvin Allen shares with guests in the Carousel Bar nearly every day—is that Walter Bergeron was trying to pay tribute in the best way he knew how to the melting-pot cultures that created the New Orleans he knew and loved. Though some of the history may be less familiar to us now, Bergeron couldn't have painted his adopted city any better had he wielded a brush at an easel with a palette splattered with paints around Jackson Square—instead of a shot glass and a cocktail shaker in one of the Crescent City's most beloved and historic hotels.

According to pretty much everybody, New Orleans took the Volstead Act less seriously than most other places. The city was blessed with an attitude born of the free and easy Mediterranean regions and perfected in the lawless buccaneer world of the Caribbean. Alcohol enjoyment would be high up on anybody's list of New Orleans (non) guilty pleasures. During the golden age before the introduction of Prohibition in 1919, the city was awash in spirits—both the kind that came off ships from Europe and the islands to the south and the kind that arrived on barges and rafts on the Mississippi from the wild hinterland of America. Some days along the city's riverfront, it must have seemed whiskey had decided to make New Orleans its home away from home.

For quite a few years, most historians even thought New Orleans had created the name "cocktail," allegedly one of many French words (*coquetier,* or egg cup) mangled by loutish, newly arrived, soon-to-be Americans. That theory is mostly abandoned now by all but the city's tour guides, yet the reality is that some of America's best and best-known cocktails hailed from this polyglot metropolis near the mouth of the Mississippi. For many (including the Louisiana Legislature), the Sazerac is the city's signature cocktail, taking its name from the Sazerac Pere et Fils cognac once used in its proper making. Others could point to the Ramos Gin Fizz, the Absinthe Suissesse, and the Roffignac as heady parts of the New Orleans contribution to cocktail culture. Still, these drinks that required care to make and sophistication to enjoy had largely faded from the local drinking scene by the time Walter Bergeron started testing and tasting pre-Prohibition combinations in the Monteleone's pre–Carousel Lobby Bar.

The villain, for those who care about alcohol and/or New Orleans, was Prohibition. The Eighteenth Amendment pushed into passage by the temperance movement— followed quickly by the Volstead Act that established federal enforcement—took a large blunt instrument to many of America's alcohol-driven activities. Today, we can point to Prohibition as starter fuel for the spread of organized crime syndicates that kept so many otherwise law-abiding citizens supplied with beer, wine, and spirits. The Twenty-First Amendment ended Prohibition in 1933 (the only amendment ever fashioned to end another), by which time Franklin D. Roosevelt had moved into the White House and was focused on battling the Great Depression.

Lobby of the Hotel Monteleone. The Historic New Orleans Collection, Gift of Mrs. Eleanor G. Burke, 2012.0238.15.

Still, the damage had been done. Hundreds of alcohol producers, including famous distilleries, wineries, and breweries, had shut their doors, having been unable to survive on the limited production allowed by the government. And a consumer base forced to exist on "bathtub gin" and other poorly made spirits had lost all familiarity with the

Lobby Bar, Hotel Monteleone. The Charles L. Franck Studio Collection at The Historic New Orleans Collection, 1979.325.4557.

superior products and great cocktails that had existed in the previous era. In short, there wasn't much of the good stuff to be had, and bartenders spent a good deal of their time disguising inferior ingredients with fruit juices and sugar.

Because Walter Bergeron is such a mystery, we don't have any record of him speaking about any of this. We'd love to have some eloquent speech about being mad as hell and not going to *shake* it anymore (yes—another pun plotted and planned for) but we don't. Instead of a speech, we have a cocktail. Almost everything we know about Walter, in fact, comes from exploring his only true legacy, the Vieux Carré.

As many savvy New Orleanians might suspect, anyone with the surname "Bergeron" is less likely to hail from the city than from the bayou-crossed Louisiana parishes to the south and west. Indeed, that is the case for Walter, as tracked down a few years ago by a researcher whose name (Cheryl Charming) is almost as intriguing as her job description (bartender and author). Working on her book *The Cocktail Companion,* Ms. Charming found Walter Bergeron especially fascinating, perhaps because so little is known about him. She determined that he was born in 1889 in the small Cajun town of Thibodaux on Bayou Lafourche. Interestingly, both his father and his mother were only thirteen years old at the time of his birth, so it is perhaps not surprising that the marriage didn't last. Walter grew up to be short and stocky, unlike his siblings, who were tall and lean. Like many from small-town/rural south Louisiana, Bergeron found himself drawn to New Orleans, presumably by the lure of gainful employment. Arriving in 1907, the twenty-year-old took little time to locate his place behind a bar. Cheryl Charming uncovered census and city directory records placing him at the Hotel Monteleone by the end of World War I in 1918, the fateful year before Prohibition took effect.

An experienced bar manager by this time, Bergeron was actually hired to manage a cigar store instead. Still, questions persist as to whether the United Cigar Store at the corner of Baronne and Gravier across wide Canal Street from the French Quarter was actually more a speakeasy than cigar shop. We know he was arrested in 1924, having been accused of possessing a gambling device known as a "punch board." It takes little imagination to picture alcohol sales liberally mixed in with cigars and gambling. In fact, while no proof exists, these elements also point to his possible familiarity with the local Mafia crime family, which was just beginning to gain sway over a fiefdom that would eventually encompass the entire Gulf Coast. The good news for Bergeron's career was that with the end of Prohibition the Monteleone family could reopen the Lobby Bar at its hotel on Royal Street. And they can hardly be blamed if one of the first things they installed there was Walter Bergeron.

"He was a simple man and, I think, a good guy," says Charming, whose efforts to research the drink's creator stretched over ten years and included locating his elderly son and grandson, both named Klebert. "He just went to work every day and came home to raise children pretty much on his own, with a little help from his sister. When I finally met them, no family member knew he created the Vieux Carré or even worked at the Monteleone."

When son Klebert recalled his dad shortly before his own death in 2014, he spoke of visiting the hotel bar in 1940, when he was ten. In New Orleans, there was nothing wrong with kids spending time with fathers, or for that matter mothers, in establishments serving alcohol. Specifically, Klebert remembered spotting a boy who looked his own age playing around on the bar floor with a red toy fire truck. He waited until the boy walked away before approaching the shiny truck. Before he could start to play, however, his father warned him to leave it alone. It belonged to the hotel owner's son.

By the time of his return to the hotel, we gather that Bergeron and his family were living in the Lower Ninth Ward—on the lengthy extension of a street that started in the French Quarter before passing north through the neighborhoods called Marigny and Bywater. We don't know if he rented or owned his domicile. We certainly don't know when or why he again left the bar serving the iconic cocktail he'd created, only that he left in the mid-1940s. It's quite possible he simply got offered more money. Bergeron started mixing drinks at the old Sazerac Bar in the Central Business District—the same building that had once housed Henry Ramos's famous Stag Saloon., which was the pre-Prohibition home of the Ramos Gin Fizz, even though the drink, and indeed Henry Ramos himself, were later associated with the Roosevelt Hotel. It was at the Roosevelt that the mixologist met Governor Huey "Kingfish" Long, who spread the drink's fame far beyond the Louisiana state line. Meanwhile, Bergeron died of a heart attack during a trip to the grocery store in 1947, a few days before Mardi Gras.

In his 1937 book *Famous New Orleans Drinks & How to Mix 'Em,* published while Bergeron was still working at the hotel, Stanley Clisby Arthur gives instructions for making the Vieux Carré. He describes it as a drink Bergeron "takes special pride in mixing" not only because it was his creation, but because he believed it to be an "honor to the famed Vieux Carré, that part of old New Orleans where the antique shops and the iron lace balconies give sightseers a glimpse into the romance of another day."

We can also thank Arthur, though we can't quite trust him on certain facts and figures, for giving us the earliest printed suggestion that Bergeron, in the creation of his cocktail, was paying homage to his city first and foremost by choosing ingredients that reflected its most important influences. As he was working in the French Quarter, he made certain to include French components, from the world-famous brandy produced (and named for) the region of Cognac to the liqueur known as Bénédictine.

During Bergeron's active years, the French Quarter was also home to a vibrant population from Italy, including many immigrants from Sicily, Calabria, and the rest of the impoverished south. He paid tribute to their many contributions (led off, naturally, by the Hotel Monteleone itself) by including sweet vermouth, a taste beloved in classic, now-rediscovered Italian drinks like the Negroni. Then, too, since the beginning of the twentieth century, some of the forces at play in New Orleans had come from the "American side" of Canal Street, giving the old French Creole families a literal run for their money. These newer arrivals from the interior of America had probably acquired a taste for whiskey, be it from Kentucky, Tennessee, or much farther north in Canada. Rye was often their spirit of choice, so rye went into the Vieux Carré as well.

Quite a few pre-Prohibition cocktails drew complexity from one ingredient known as "bitters," so Bergeron for some reason decided he liked what happened when he added *two* kinds of bitters. Both products had roots in the Caribbean, an area with long, sad links to the slave trade but also to embracing the port of New Orleans as its doorway to the entire United States. The clearer of the two histories belongs to Angostura bitters from Trinidad, an ever-popular import that could be spotted behind bars all over town. More complex, but also more locally beloved, was Peychaud's bitters—produced in New Orleans, its name a profound link to the very beginnings of the city's history. Antoine Amédée Peychaud, an apothecary by trade, was actually born on the French Caribbean island of Saint-Domingue, now Creole *patois*-speaking Haiti. It was the bloody slave rebellion there from 1791 to 1804 that sent thousands, both white and Black, escaping by ship to New Orleans, nearly doubling the population while exoticizing every aspect of the city's culture with layered seasonings, mesmerizing rhythms, and the practice of voodoo.

Thus, when head bartender Walter Bergeron told Stanley Clisby Arthur that the origins of his cocktail were the origins of his adopted city, the writer had every reason to pay attention. Immigration was on Bergeron's mind, clearly, and not only the immigration of cultures, food, drink, and ideas but the dramatic influx of *people*. The early days of New Orleans were about *nothing* so much as immigration, a fact that it would be very hard to miss if you were tending bar in a hotel named "Lion Mountain"—in Sicilian.

A SICILIAN SUCCESS STORY

The French Quarter—the New Orleans neighborhood in which Antonio Montelone chose to build his grand hotel—has always been a sucker for a good yarn. It's heard millions of them since its creation by French colonizers and rebuilding by Spanish opportunists, and it's told its visitors a few million more. But while Antonio understood this from the soles of his shoes (more about shoes in a minute) to the top of his cap as he went from repairing shoes to hosting dignitaries, he knew his own story would be a better yarn than any the most fact-averse tourist carriage driver could concoct.

A word, first, though, about the business Antonio Monteleone chose to enter, in which his descendants would still be working decades and generations later. Some simply call it the "hotel business," though it's now more often known as the "hospitality industry." To many veterans, it's just "hotels"—as in, "I work in hotels" or "I've been in hotels for twenty-five years." Call it what you will, it's hard work with long hours and with the pickiest bosses the world has ever invented: i.e., each and every guest. In some weird way, if you're a person with the right gifts (the hospitality gene it's often called by those who have it), you become big by making yourself become small. How else can you explain the hospitality offered by those who know the business best? "What can we bring you?" "Anything else you'd like?" "If there's anything you need, here's my personal number." Essentially, in the hospitality industry, those who become kings are the best at becoming servants. And they don't even have to think about it. Somehow, between Sicily and New Orleans, Antonio Monteleone came to understand this truth better than anybody else on his ship.

Antonio was anything but alone. In the final two or three decades of the nineteenth century, immigration drove growth in America. The word went forth to every nook and cranny on earth: "Come to America." This phrase launched a thousand ships: "The streets are paved with gold." In Sicily, at this time a struggling southern outpost of a cobbled-together republic of many identities, many loyalties, and many dialects, this promise rang louder than church bells. Antonio may have heard it as far back as he could remember. Some relatives were already in America, some probably in New Orleans—writing home about a French Quarter that looked more like Spain and sounded more like Palermo or Messina. Historians now tell us that, by 1890, there were thirty thousand "Italians" in New Orleans. Most were from Sicily, and most lived in the French Quarter, gathered around the Catholic church they called Santa Maria but which everybody else in town knew, tellingly, as "St. Mary's Italian."

The only trick, for Sicilians, as for any other immigrant or immigrant group, was making a living. Yes, it helped to band together. It never hurt to have relatives or friends who spoke not only your language but the dialect preferred in your village. All this mattered especially when it came time to get married. It was then that parents, grandparents, and godparents gathered around and pressured you to marry this one or that one. It would be good to understand each other's language. Often the young man and woman loved the same foods, the same dances, the same music. They might have been eyeing each other since First Communion at St. Mary's Italian. That was, after all, the way it usually worked. And the next generation, speaking better English and with a few more pennies in its pocket, could launch itself on the adventure known as Life in America.

Most accounts of the Hotel Monteleone's history have Antonio immigrating from "Italy" or "Sicily, Italy," but at least a couple have him hailing from "Contessa, Italy." This actually sets his birthplace as a town, or *commune,* south of Palermo, that sprawling, crowded city along the north coast of Sicily. Contessa Entellina, the town's full name, is actually one of only three ethnic communities of *Arbëreshe* in Sicily, who still speak the Albanian language of their origin and carefully preserve aspects of that culture, from their Eastern Orthodox Christianity to native costumes, music, and dancing. The population of the town goes back to the 1400s, though by Antonio's time the most popular thing to do in Contessa was head to America. Not surprisingly, with the lure of having relatives established in

Antonio Monteleone. Courtesy Hotel Monteleone.

a place, many immigrants from the town headed for New Orleans. A website devoted to the genealogy of Contessa Entellina shows many requests about ancestors from long-settled New Orleans families. An internet list of popular surnames in the town would be entirely familiar to New

Orleanians, including Chetta, Vaccaro, Tardo, Lala, Scramuzza, and Sciambra.

Before coming to America, Antonio was either, depending on what you're reading, a "cobbler by trade" or a "nobleman" who had inherited a successful shoe factory in Sicily. The only thing the contradictory stories have in common, besides Sicily of course, is a focus on footwear. Nonetheless, Antonio arrived in New Orleans in the 1880s, throwing in his lot with relatives who owned two different shoe repair shops on Royal Street. Eventually he opened his own cobbler shop and quickly (suggesting he had more startup capital than the average Sicilian immigrant) grew that into a shoe factory. Initially he bought property in an area pressed against the French Quarter, now known as the Faubourg Marigny (in honor of gambling womanizer Bernard de Marigny de Mandeville). To pay off gambling debts, Marigny was forced to sell his estate holdings overlooking the Mississippi River, and the land was subdivided into a neighborhood. On a side note, Marigny did invent (and name) the dice game "craps," calling it *les crapeaux* because men playing it squatted like toads.

Eventually, life for Antonio, his wife Sophia, and their children became centered on Royal Street. He not only bought the family's home on the thoroughfare but started building his hotel empire in 1886, first by running the small Hotel Victor above the shop where he was selling shoes and then taking over the sixty-four-room Commercial Hotel. The latter was charging guests a dollar a night in those days, with an extra charge if they wanted a bath. Even at those rates, in a time of smaller Mom-and-Pop hotels, inns, and pensions, the Commercial was true to its name. It was one of the few small hotels to place ads in the *Daily Picayune,* going up against larger advertisers like the Hotel Grunewald across Canal Street, which would later become the Roosevelt, then the Fairmont, and finally the Roosevelt again. Over the first few years of the twentieth century, Antonio's hotel complex expanded several times, success breeding even greater success. In 1909, the combined prop-

Opposite: Architectural drawing of the Hotel Monteleone (postcard). The Historic New Orleans Collection, Gift of Mrs. Eleanor G. Burke, 2012.0238.31.

erty got a proud new name, written in red lights above the highest French Quarter rooftops—the Hotel Monteleone. It is a beacon seen from many parts and many streets of the French Quarter to this day.

In the final years before his death in 1913, Antonio Monteleone clearly had legacy—and family—on his mind. Having the family name above one extraordinary hotel seemed the starting block rather than the finish line of such a grand project. And the time seemed right, with the entire country celebrating a generally opulent period before Europe crashed into the trauma of World War I. New Orleans, thankfully, shared in the general good fortune, finally performing much the role envisioned by Thomas Jefferson when he carried out the Louisiana Purchase. The city was a port through which goods could flow out from the heartland of America, more often by riverboat or barge than by train, to the burgeoning economies of not only Europe but Central and South America. Many goods streamed into New Orleans as well, especially the tropical fruits that inspired one cynical journalist to call Louisiana "the northernmost banana republic." Despite any criticism the city's success might attract, people and money kept coming to New Orleans. And both had a tendency to find their way to the Monteleone hotel.

Antonio's faith in the future of New Orleans was unshakeable, and for him that meant faith in the future of the French Quarter as the heart of the city's tourism and business travel. With that future in mind, and well aware that the neighborhood had burned to the ground twice in the distant past, Antonio made fireproofing part of the construction of each new real estate acquisition leading to each new wing of his signature property. Other businesses came and went as the long-neglected neighborhood took on greater style, comfort, and importance, an evolution that wouldn't bear fruit for decades. But Antonio was one of the few visionaries who saw the Quarter's destiny on the distant horizon and built a business to be ready for it.

There was one segment of local society that Monteleone showed no interest in meeting, but of course they showed up at his door anyway—the Sicilian-controlled Mafia. The thing organized crime did best—providing money for growth while holding onto a piece of the action—

was at one level what the hotelier could have used most, especially as his luxurious new hotel took shape in his final years. By all accounts, however, Antonio snubbed the local mob bosses (the hotel's fireproofing might have had a second motive) and somehow lived to tell the tale. He informed at least one listener that he was accustomed to ignoring the mob after growing up in Sicily, and that he understood it would be "more difficult possibly for others, who have not heretofore had the experience." Antonio (now known universally as "Mr. Monteleone") had accomplished what perhaps no other Sicilian of his time had managed to do: joined the elite bankers, brokers, and import-export owners who ran the city year to year. He even was allowed to participate in Carnival as a member of the blue-blooded Rex court.

Though nearly always present at his hotel and ready to welcome VIP guests, Antonio also loved to travel to the Europe he had left to make his fortune—the Europe of grand hotels owned by grand hotel families that had inspired his own vision, the Europe of magnificent dining rooms he might wish for his own properties, although aware that most Americans were a different breed of traveler. It was on one of his trips, in 1913, in a German spa town called Bad Nauheim, that Antonio breathed his last. He was fifty-eight years old. "Pioneer shoe manufacturer, hotel proprietor, banker, promoter and man of affairs generally," wrote the *Daily Picayune*. "Mr. Monteleone held a conspicuous place in the public life of New Orleans and everybody knew him either personally or by reputation. His rise to financial greatness is a story of ingenious struggle, tireless energy and the close application of natural talents to a high purpose."

Antonio had envisioned the hotel's future as a mission for his family. Sadly, his three sons were too young to take over at the time of his death, so management fell into the proven hands of the manager who served as his executor— James D. Kenney, who was also married to his daughter Stella. Unfortunately, Monteleone's wife and two of his sons, Antonio Jr. and William, would pass away over the next decades. Under Kenney and Antonio's surviving son, Frank, the Monteleone continued its tradition of land acquisition and expansion into other construction. "Magnificent fourteen-story annex recently completed," boasted a promotional piece in 1931, even after the Crash of 1929 and the beginnings of the Great Depression. "The rooms are large and airy, having both tubs and shower baths and are also provided with running ice water for the convenience of our guests."

Several more serious renovations further launched the Hotel Monteleone, each adding elements that helped it keep a competitive edge. These occurred first under Frank Monteleone, then under his son William, known as Billy, and then under *his* son Billy Jr. Within the family, there was always some relief when a renovation was completed but never a sense that it would prove to be the final touch. The Monteleone seemed to embody the business maxim that if you're standing still, you're falling behind.

It is true, nonetheless, that each renovation was a tad more complicated and difficult because of the very success Antonio himself had predicted for the French Quarter. There was, increasingly year after year, a death match being fought between powers seeking all things new in the name of profit and those seeking to preserve all things old in the name of tradition. The latter, when embodied by a family like the Monteleones, believed that in the French Quarter, new had to coexist beside old, timely next to timeless, in order for the city's historic center of tourism to thrive. In the end, no one had understood this balance better than Antonio Monteleone.

AS THE BAR TURNS

No people travel with eyes and ears as wide open as hotel people, and so it was with the Monteleones. How else do you think they created the Carousel Bar to serve Walter Bergeron's Vieux Carré cocktail beginning in the late 1940s? Walter, as we know, died before setting foot in the lounge that would carry his fame (and his cocktail) into the present day. For him, work was done through long hours in the Lobby Bar, a part of so many hotels that encourage people meeting people for a drink before or after anything else. That's what the place was forever called, in any hotel that had one: The Lobby Bar.

The Carousel Lounge in its heyday. The Historic New Orleans Collection, Gift of Mr. Gary Henershott, 1983.222.12.

Then, on one of their postwar business trips, the Monteleones who took over the property and expanded it tirelessly after Antonio's death saw an innovative bar—one that rotated. Running on a single motor, the bar turned in place all hours that it was open for business. Or, more pre-

Early postcard of the Carousel Lounge. Courtesy Hotel Monteleone.

cisely, the twenty-five bar *stools* turned on two thousand rollers driven by a one-quarter horsepower motor beneath the floor around a stationary service area. Some patrons surely joked, then as now, that it just wasn't right to punish bewildered drunks by continually changing their scenery. But the Monteleones loved the idea. It was at least a great gimmick, and since the idea was for the bar to turn *very slowly*, the trips around shouldn't leave anybody seasick.

Seen in historical context, what became the Carousel Bar was simply one more profit center and one more talking

View of the Central Business District from atop the Hotel Monteleone. The Charles L. Franck Studio Collection at The Historic New Orleans Collection, 1979.325.6778.

point, one more reason to stay at the Monteleone over the new hotels rising up around it in the French Quarter, in the Central Business District, and out along graceful St. Charles Avenue in the Garden District. Along the way, the Carousel became a favored watering hole of authors who made a special point of staying at the hotel, a list including William Faulkner, Tennessee Williams, Truman Capote, Richard Ford, and Winston Groom of *Forrest Gump* fame.

Other notable bar patrons have included Michael Jordan, Dennis Quaid, Gregg Allman, and Sally Struthers.

Several changes in décor came along over the decades, with a major redesign in 1992 adding the current carousel top. Fiber optics were installed in the ceiling to create the illusion of stars in the night sky, along with one special shooting star that crossed the room at regular intervals. An additional adjoining space came eventually, featuring a piano for entertaining. That space and that piano, for better or worse, stayed in one place.

Hotel Monteleone poster, detailing important events in the hotel's history. The Historic New Orleans Collection, Gift of John H. Lawrence, 2011.0175.1.

CHAPTER TWO

THE BIG FOUR

RYE WHISKEY

Though he left no record of thinking deeply on the subject, Walter Bergeron's selection of rye whiskey to represent the American influence on New Orleans would prove to be an inspired choice. After all, within a few years of fighting the British about independence, Americans were busy fighting each other about whiskey. And it was rye that put the "whiskey" in the Whiskey Rebellion.

However, since we don't have Bergeron's thoughts, we can imagine he might possibly have had a different link to the past in mind. He might have chosen to include rye whiskey because of its symbolic role in the New Orleans–born Sazerac. The earliest recipes for this cocktail, of course, feature the cognac that supplied its name—Sazerac de Forge et Fils. Within a few decades, however, many bartenders around New Orleans had taken to mixing Sazeracs with rye whiskey instead. It might have been a simple substitution made for expediency, a matter of supply and demand, or even a single customer's taste preference. But it also may have reflected the impact of *les Americains,* the once-hated newcomers from the interior who had made their way to this European-seeming city that had recently become part of the young United States.

By today's laws, rye whiskey has to be made from a mash of at least 51 percent rye (a grass grown as a grain similar to wheat and used to make flour for bread as well as beer, whiskey, and vodka), though other ingredients in the whiskey can include corn and malted barley. It is distilled to a maximum of 160 U.S. proof (that's an intimidating 80 percent alcohol by volume—a measurement expressed as "ABV") and then aged in charred barrels built with new oak. When rye has been aged in oak for at least two years and not blended with any other spirit, it can be marketed, logically and legally enough, as "straight rye whiskey."

The trouble, if you'd asked small-scale rye farmers in western Pennsylvania around 1791, was the U.S. Constitution. It actually allowed the federal government to tax domestic products, and not just those hoity-toity imports like the Châteauneuf-du-Pape that rich landowner Thomas Jefferson had delivered to his estate at Monticello. This tax applied to the small batches of rye whiskey that western farmers made with leftover grain, sometimes to drink but most importantly to sell after it made a difficult trek over the mountains to big cities in the east. President George Washington of eastern Virginia thought the tax was a marvelous idea to help the new country with its staggering debts, as did Treasury Secretary Alexander Hamilton of New York City. Looking back, it's safe to say these two otherwise-smart gentlemen had no idea.

The whiskey makers rebelled. In scenes that resemble

the later battles between moonshiners and "revenuers" during Prohibition, they took to shooting at men given the task of collecting the taxes. Some of those men were even locals, chosen for their recognizable faces and, unfortunately, their familiar home addresses. The rebels didn't have to burn down too many of these homes before the collectors began looking for some other line of work—and George Washington started looking for a way out. What he settled on was part carrot and part stick. Against the tax protesters in western Pennsylvania, and their less numerous counterparts west of the mountains in Maryland, Virginia, North Carolina, South Carolina, and Georgia, President Washington raised a large army. He had the good sense to ignore the frontier state of Kentucky, since no one there would be talked into enforcing the law or attempting to collect the whiskey tax. The president, despite the hot-headed urgings of Hamilton, also offered to negotiate. It was the second tack that eventually brought peace beyond the mountains.

The Whiskey Rebellion, in general, proved that the United States considered imposing domestic excise taxes part of its constitutional powers and that it would send its armies to collect them, if necessary. Still, the uproar from the whiskey makers lasted as an echo for years, gathering force around the candidacy of Thomas Jefferson in the first true American political campaign in 1800. Jefferson defeated the more tax-friendly John Adams and, as promised, abolished the federal whiskey tax. In a quite separate move, of course, he later signed off on the Louisiana Purchase, setting up New Orleans as the port to ship whiskey and many other American products to appreciative customers overseas. At least some of that rye entered the city by barge or raft on the Mississippi River, and never quite made it out.

"The first error," Jefferson said in a postmortem for the whiskey tax promoted by his bitter rival, Hamilton, "was to pass it. The second was to enforce it. And the third to make it the means of splitting this Union."

Somewhat typically of New Orleans, the city and its bartenders would cling to their fascination with rye long after its popularity, and even its availability, had faded dramatically. Within a few years of the Whiskey Rebellion, spirit distillers in Kentucky and Tennessee began convincing many drinkers that the sweeter spirit they sold as bourbon made a more satisfying sip. Many went so far as to start using bourbon instead of rye in the then-new collection of cocktails like the Old Fashioned, the Manhattan, and the whiskey sour. As usual in matters of flavor profile, the flavor people got used to tasting would be the flavor that won. Prohibition was the last straw for many rye producers, injuring everyone's alcohol business and delivering fatal blows to an industry already struggling. It wasn't long before drinkers heard the words "rye whiskey" and thought only of the spirit of that name from Canada, thus overlooking an important, or at least very colorful, chapter in early American history.

Rye making, and rye makers, never disappeared entirely, though. Bergeron and other fans of the Sazerac in New Orleans always managed to get their hands on enough of the stuff to get by. They showed their support for the drier, and undeniably intended taste, that rye brings to any cocktail it decides to join, as contrasted and even opposed to the sweeter taste delivered by bourbon. A handful of brands, like Old Overholt, managed to stick around after Prohibition. And of course, Bergeron probably wouldn't have included rye in his Vieux Carré recipe had he fore-seen difficulty with the supply. Irony of ironies, by the late 1960s, even the most revered Pennsylvania brands like Old Overholt found themselves being made in Kentucky.

The craft cocktail renaissance has been a godsend to rye whiskey, as a spirit if not always as a business. With this reawakening, mostly brought about by bartenders com-mitted to making traditional drinks with their traditional ingredients, big liquor companies bought into the notion of expanding their product line. Thus, we now have rye whiskeys from the likes of Campari Group (Wild Turkey Rye), Diageo (George Dickel and Bulleit), Beam Suntory (Old Overholt and, naturally, Jim Beam Rye), and even the Sazerac Company (Thomas H. Handy, Col. E. H. Taylor, and the relatively new Sazerac Rye). Perhaps more import-ant to the whiskey's image, any number of small-batch pro-ducers have emerged in the early twenty-first century, pro-ducing what amounts to a craft whiskey for making craft cocktails. Many states are witnessing a rye revival, though no area with more enthusiasm than western Pennsylvania. Pittsburgh is considered the heart of this rebirth of rye.

Perhaps the most ironic of these new makers is George Washington's very own estate at Mount Vernon in Virginia, overlooking the Potomac not far from the Atlantic Ocean. In the estate's reconstructed distillery, successors to the followers of the president who sent an army to quash the Whiskey Rebellion today make a small-batch whiskey similar to the one the Father of Our Country used to make. Like so many others in his day, he made the iconic spirit to sell, not merely for himself to sip. As history records, Washington "beat" the rye whiskey rebels. But perhaps they won in the long run.

COGNAC

Viticulture means, specifically, the agriculture of growing grapes to make wine. But it also, more broadly, posits the existence of an audience—a *culture,* if you will—to buy and consume the finished product. A business. Though archaeologists have found earlier evidence of wine in Europe, the Middle East, and even China, the origin of wine as a trade is generally located in first-century Roman Gaul, in the region named Burdigala, which morphed (happily) into Bordeaux. The evidence suggests that long before Burgundy got into the trade in the late second century, Germany's Mosel Valley in the late third century, or the Loire Valley in the fifth century, viticulture had taken hold not far from Bordeaux, around the future village of Cognac.

This development was no accident. A Roman emperor named Probus had defeated the threatening Germanic tribes, restoring borders at the Rhine and Danube, and then built protective walls around much of Gaul. Now he wanted the land he'd protected so expensively to be worth something, so he lifted all restrictions on growing grapes for wine. The Roman province of Gaul, along with a similar protectorate along the Danube, was about to discover its agricultural *raison d'être*.

In twentieth-century New Orleans, had Walter Bergeron ignored the first fifteen hundred years of Cognac winemaking, he would have been on solid ground. The French product, seen from the other side of an ocean, wasn't especially distinguished. And since Cognac rested near the ocean, the focus of its trade had always been on shipping to England, Flanders in today's Belgium, the Netherlands, and beyond. Over time, challenges presented by long sea voyages took their toll on the reputation of wines from Cognac, and other regions in France were quick to take up the slack. What Cognac needed was a wine with a much higher alcohol content, so it could travel better out to a waiting world. Fortunately for Cognac, other parts of the world had been working on precisely that.

The Arab world in particular had been working on distillation as the next step after fermentation. Fermentation happened in nature, as many had observed for millennia—but distillation required science and technology. Applying heat to not only reduce and raise the alcohol level in fermented fruit juice (grapes, but also apples, peaches, and most other fruits) but to purify what remained after a trip through tubing was a technique that came to France by way of exploration and experimentation in the Middle East. Yes, there had been progress made in this process by Greeks and Romans, but the actual technique for extracting the essence of liquids via evaporation and condensation wasn't perfected until the sixteenth century. Distillation came to Holland around the same time as France, its end product being given the name *brandewijn* "burnt wine." The shortened word "brandy" stuck, scoring one for the Dutch. Arab scientists, however, scored at least two for their inventions: The device that worked such magic evolved from *al-anbiq* to alembic, and the magic itself from *al-kuhul* to alcohol.

In one of those marriages made in alcohol heaven—it turned out that the unexciting wines produced in the Cognac region made one of the best brandies anyone has ever tasted. And the high-alcohol stuff traveled well. Before long, many parts of the winemaking world were producing some variation on brandy. But in the French method of naming to emphasize place of origin, the name "cognac" came to evoke the highest aspirations of both the fermentation and distillation arts. Many Frenchmen let the romance run away with them, calling cognac *eau de vie,* meaning "water of life."

Cognac came into its own in the 1700s, as consumers—especially in countries that traded with France via the bustling port of La Rochelle—came to appreciate the product's uniqueness. Virtually every other brand being made in France ran the liquid through the still time after time to refine it, but the producers in Cognac decided to do so only twice. This technique preserved the flavor tones of the original wine, instead of turning it into a far less interesting fortified wine. By then, as well, Cognac had developed its system of negotiants, trading houses that pushed forward with the special brandy into market after market. The Dutch became an especially enthusiastic audience, with many Cognac families sending a son to live in Amsterdam and deal with their best customers directly. It was the success of such tactics in Holland and elsewhere, even in the Americas as those colonies developed and eventually won independence, that helps explains Cognac's dominance in the international market.

When all this was happening, two of the three most established cognac brands began their production and marketing efforts. In 1715 a young trader named Jean Martell moved to France from the English Channel island of Guernsey to be closer to the glorious stuff he sold. After marrying one wealthy woman and then another after being widowed, Martell founded a cognac house that would still be thriving three hundred years later, tied for third place in sales with its rival Courvoisier. Remy Martin would follow as early as 1724, its eau de vie becoming the favorite of King Louis XV. Today Remy enjoys prestige as the world's second most successful cognac house. The brandies they produced joined then-exotic food and drink products from the Americas, the West Indies, Africa, and India, offering pleasures at a price to Europe's fast-growing middle class. The fact that part of this trade often involved transporting enslaved humans from Africa to the Americas didn't seem to bother that public for at least the first century or so. "It was a very risky business," observed Jacques Peret of the University of Poitiers. "But when it worked, you won the jackpot."

In 1753 a member of an Irish brigade who had been wounded fighting for Louis XV left the army and settled in Flanders before pulling up stakes a decade later for Cognac. He had been selling the brandy successfully, so he was tempted to try blending and merchandizing his own. The

Irishman's name was Richard Hennessy. The cognac house he founded would one day be the biggest of them all.

It was at the beginning of the nineteenth century that cognac began its most over-romanticized relationship— with Napoleon Bonaparte. Napoleon, of course, was the French leader who ran up such debt from his various conquests that he decided to sell the Louisiana Territory, freshly returned from Spanish control, to the young American nation. The emperor wasn't a huge drinker but, by all accounts, had a favorite wine and spirits warehouse in Paris, run by a man named Emmanuel Courvoisier. Emmanuel's son Felix set the family up as a cognac house in the town of Jarnac and began a marketing campaign that continues to this day, placing Napoleon's image on every bottle. All the same, considering that many of Napoleon's attacks were launched against England and England remained a major buyer of cognac, most people working in the business were none too sad to see him lose to Wellington at Waterloo and depart in disgrace for exile.

One of the signature aspects of cognac culture was born in the late nineteenth century, a time when Russia,

Spain, Italy, and Germany started selling a wine-based brandy as everything from Koniac to Cogniac to Kognac. Eventually, even Mexico, Chile, and Brazil got into the fraudulent act. In response to this potential loss of market share, negotiants in the real Cognac began building huge warehouses along the Charente River and blending cognacs to create a unique house style. Out of this blending came a hierarchy based on time spent in oak barrels after distillation, the names generally stated in English in honor of their longtime best customers. The youngest were classified as VS (Very Special), having aged at least two years, followed by VSOP (Very Superior Old Pale) at four years, up to XO (Extra Old) at ten years. Since blends usually include cognacs of different ages, the designation is based on the youngest in the mix. Around the world today, cognac drinkers must be waiting to sample a rare one that's called *Hors d'âge*, meaning "beyond age." Some would argue such words apply nicely to any and all cognacs.

After the economic roller coaster that followed World War II and eventually inspired the European Union, cognac—the only brandy on earth that comes from the

Cognac region of France—remains at the head of its class, in both reputation and price. Though Asia has entered the list of its markets, the United States remains the heart of France's cognac exports. And typical of a still-young country, change here seems the only thing that's constant. VS cognacs, the youngest and least expensive, have enjoyed huge new popularity among an audience that is younger as well. With their gargantuan marketing budgets, the cognac giants have finally discovered African Americans and other demographics that were not previously front and center. And the iconic marketing picture of a person enjoying a cognac has evolved from an older white male with his fingers wrapped around a snifter by a roaring fire into a younger, less formal, and less *white* group of men and women enjoying each other's company at a throbbing nightclub.

Not coincidentally, cognac no longer has to be sipped with contemplation from a snifter (even as, ironically, *añejo* tequilas have sought to be). It can be and is mixed with ingredients old and new into a vast collection of craft cocktails. It would appear Walter Bergeron had the right idea after all.

VERMOUTH

Despite its close association with Italy, the ancient history of vermouth goes back ten thousand years and touches pretty much every continent. North America has, admittedly, come late to the party, producing in recent decades not only an argument about what vermouth actually is but some of the finest small-batch vermouths anyone has ever tasted. Most impressively, according to craft vermouth maker Adam Ford of New York City, vermouth has earned recognition as "the spirit that created America's cocktail culture."

By the time he started experimenting with what became his Vieux Carré, Walter Bergeron had been tending bar for two-going-on-three decades at the Monteleone, doing so in a city that tended to defend its traditions and reject any but minor innovations. That means he was quite familiar with vermouth in classic cocktails, whether the dry kind pioneered in southern France and used in martinis or the sweet kind originating in northern Italy and used in Manhattans. Bergeron knew the taste of traditional European vermouths, though we have no record that he was aware that the very taste was under attack. The greatest enemy vermouth would ever face was—the twentieth century.

First, there was the Great War, which like the conflict that would follow in the late 1930s destroyed much of everyday life across Europe. France and Italy suffered mightily during "the war to end all wars," meaning their economies were left in shambles. Still, in the world of vermouth, the worst blow didn't come from either world war but from the U.S. Prohibition era that fell in between. The American market for vermouth dried up when alcoholic beverages became illegal, even as the American market for other spirits like gin, rum, rye, and bourbon moved underground and, despite law enforcement's best efforts, prospered. With a focus on finding, buying, or making the primary spirit in a drink, the desire for what seemed at best a supporting actor dropped through the floorboards.

Recipes for martinis, which originally had featured vermouth as an equal partner to gin, now used barely a flourish. In the Vieux Carré cocktail, an equal amount of vermouth joins the rye and the cognac. Later, vermouth became the kind of mere suggestion that drinkers found they could easily do without. Pretty much no one drank vermouth as an aperitif anymore, so its complex flavor dropped out of sight. Drinks that used Italy's sweet vermouth, like the Manhattan and the Negroni, fell from grace. Everyone knew someone making "bathtub gin" during Prohibition, but no one ever heard of anybody bothering to make "bathtub vermouth." Overall vermouth quality dropped accordingly, along with the public's ability to care. By the postwar years, drinkers were telling bartenders to go light on the vermouth in their martinis. One cocktail historian said bartenders were trained to treat vermouth "like toxic waste." With its history reaching back thousands of years, vermouth deserved far better than it got during the twentieth century.

Like so many other spirits, especially those involving "botanicals" like bark, leaves, and fruit, vermouth came out of that long-ago debate about whether humans valued alcohol as medicine or enjoyment. In the beginning, whether that was in China or Egypt or Greece, the emphasis was on medicine, as best we can tell. There were no medicines as we know them now, not least because there was no microbial knowledge as we have it now. What there *were* were products of nature that people decided, through some primal version of trial and error, were "good" for the body. Quite often, the theories coming out of this process were incorrect. But they traveled with humanity for thousands of years, until something akin to science could put them to the test. Fermentation emerged through this early period as a process humankind couldn't prevent; distillation was a process humankind initially couldn't perform.

No one is sure where the name "vermouth" came from, though some insist it started out in German as *wermut* for wormwood. As this is the controversial part of absinthe, the part (wrongly) accused of driving drinkers mad, it obviously attracted attention. For a time, some producers argued that vermouth could only be vermouth if it had wormwood among its ten, twenty, fifty, or more flavorings, the precise formula being the essence of what is considered the "brand." Many of the twenty-first century's highest quality vermouths don't feel any need to include wormwood. The production process, going back millennia, involves starting with a neutral grape wine or unfermented wine "must" (crushed fruit), followed by the addition of alcohol and those proprietary herbs, roots, and barks. This wine, "aromatized" by the botanicals and "fortified" by the extra alcohol, is finally sweetened with either cane sugar or, for a rich golden color and taste, caramelized sugar. The two forms, represented in high profile today by Cinzano or Martini & Rossi for the sweet and Noilly Prat for the dry, emerged between the mid 1700s and the early 1800s.

By the nineteenth century, the "medicinal" tradition of vermouth and other spirits had waned, giving way to an emphasis on flavor, on drinking for pleasure. The cocktail was born, probably the practice long before the name, with vermouth a major component of cocktail after cocktail. Though it applied only to the dry variety, the celebrity image surrounding the martini helped keep the notion of vermouth alive through otherwise dark times—whether the high-profile imbibers were Nick and Nora Charles in *The Thin Man* movies or larger-than-life personalities like Ernest Hemingway and Humphrey Bogart in their own time. Among men in particular, magazines like *Esquire* made the martini seem part of every self-respecting male's lifestyle, an alcoholic reality later reflected via retro television series like *Mad Men*. Still, no man real or imagined made quite the fuss about a martini that cinema spy James Bond did: "a medium dry martini, lemon peel. Shaken, not stirred."

Vermouth has enjoyed a rediscovery by bartenders and drinkers and a renaissance among producers during the "craft cocktail" twenty-first century. As bartenders, in New Orleans and elsewhere, reached back to the way "people used to drink," they have discovered that vermouth was seldom far from the bar counter. And that included both the sweet and the dry. Even in this age of fruit juice–based drinks and glasses full of bubbles, the market has grown for generally stiff cocktails that no longer work so hard at diminishing the flavor of vermouth. This trend has been driven farther than anyone would have predicted by the launch of artisanal vermouth producers in quite a few states. These thrive, first and foremost, by doing a more careful job of production. But they also take their orders from a local or regional audience that embraces the very idea of local or regional botanicals. These days, it's possible to prepare a collection of "identical" Vieux Carrés that not only arguably taste better than one made by Walter Bergeron himself but that taste wildly different from each other.

BÉNÉDICTINE

They all wanted to believe him, to buy into the story Alexandre Le Grand was telling—even in 1863, an age that felt modern enough that skepticism already seemed cool. At the very least, he got to spin the yarn over and over, until perhaps even he started to believe it. British celebrity chef Jamie Oliver certainly seems to, to hear him share the main points a century and a half later.

"For over two hundred fifty years the monks distilled their drink, until the angry mobs of the French Revolution disturbed the religious status quo," says Oliver. "Having reached Normandy, the revolting peasants were grabbing anything to help them topple the monarchy, so the monks buried their relics and the recipe book to protect them. The recipe and the distillation lay unseen for decades, until Alexandre Le Grand bought a plot of land with some buildings near the beach in Fecamp. He also acquired a library in one of the buildings and, quietly browsing through the collection of books, stumbled upon the ancient tome that included the drink recipe." With one additional word, the chef might be telling us all we really need to know about Le Grand. Seeking a job description to explain this famous story, he calls the Frenchman an "entrepreneur."

Since 1863, many have come to doubt the tale. They know Le Grand developed a tasty liqueur along the lines of Grand Marnier and Cointreau, which had delivered multigenerational wealth and influence to families that owned the formulas and produced them. Why not make one more—and theme it around the nearby ruins of a twelfth-century Benedictine abbey? In fact, why not credit the recipe to a monk named Dom Bernardo Vincelli, reputed to have first started making the stuff back in 1510?

Le Grand's stroke of genius, or maybe simply his stroke of fortune, lay in the fact that his public was ready to believe him, based on the facts they already knew. Liqueurs had started appearing all across Europe at the time Le

Grand spotlighted. They were, after all, easily made compared to many other food and wine products finding their way into national and regional economies. All a fellow, monk or otherwise, had to do was steep herbs, plants, seeds, and fruits, then mix the concoction with spirits or a fortified wine like brandy. In keeping with their times, such liqueurs were explained and understood as elixirs, perhaps even possessing healing or magical powers. Who wouldn't trust the monks? They did, after all, possess more education than just about anyone within two hundred miles. And they were holy men besides. Today, a fifth generation of the Le Grand family is hoping we'll embrace a good story as uncritically as the people around Fecamp did in Alexandre's day.

However it was that he came upon the formula, the founder ended up experimenting at great length. He prepared batch after batch in a small pot that the family still keeps on display, finally deciding to add a little sweetness to a recipe calling for no fewer than twenty-seven ingredients. Of course, then as now, the family kept the recipe a secret, though teasing us with the mention of hyssop, myrrh, aloe, lemon rind, and Angelica seeds. To cover his steps even more, Alexandre steeped and distilled his mixture with brandy in five batches, then let it age in oak casks for two years. The result found an audience around Fecamp right away. Bénédictine has stayed popular around the world to this day.

Remaining controlled by its founding family was no small trick for the spirit, not least because Alexandre married twice and produced nineteen surviving children. With the flourish shown by founders of dynasties throughout history, the Frenchman granted the entire enterprise to his four oldest sons and their descendants in his will. Today that number of descendants has topped three thousand people, though no more than forty are actual stockholders and work in the company. The rest get invited to a family reunion now and again. Interestingly, the religious order tracing its origins to St. Benedict is also a minority shareholder, presumably for giving the liqueur its blessing from Rome.

Back in the day, when Alexandre was just seeking the order's approval—both for the recipe and the story he was starting to tell—he did three things now considered unusual but essential to the family business. And to hear fifth-generation Alain Le Grand talk about these things in the family's palace, you have no choice but to be impressed with the "modernity" of the vision. The first was putting the image of the abbey front and center. He knew he had a good product, but it was that link to the history of the local abbey that separated Bénédictine from its numerous competitors. Alexandre spent a lot of money on that image at the start, say his heirs, and the truth is that he (and they) have never stopped. His second modern move was to trademark the name, label, and bottle in every market the company entered, forbidding their use by others for, well, practically any product. Only the Russians managed to skate around this registration after the Bolshevik Revolution, the heirs say, allowing them to sell a truly inferior liqueur by the much-protected brand number. And finally, for all the pride Alexandre took in France and being French, he knew from the start his future was in export markets. Today, a full 85 percent of the Bénédictine made in Fecamp goes to 213 markets abroad.

People of the area no doubt worried about Alexandre's sanity when he talked about policies that wouldn't become popular in some quarters for almost a century. They knew he'd lost his mind when he went on a now-fabled buying and building spree. Even his wives and children tried to stop him, apparently with little success. He blew a fortune on collecting wooden and plastic saints, tapestries, enamel reliquaries, and ancient chests and keys from all over western Europe, then proceeded to have workers construct an ornate and vast Renaissance palace to house it all. Le Grand had two palaces built, in fact—one to serve as a museum and what we'd now call a tourist attraction, the other as the Bénédictine factory. This "factory palace" wasn't finished until 1876, and the debt wasn't retired until the next Le Grand generation.

In addition to two world wars that saw some of their worst battles on French soil, the first half of the twentieth century was not kind to Bénédictine. The first, or Great War, spilled directly into the Russian Revolution and the loss of an important drinking market after that trademark defeat. And that spilled directly into Prohibition in the

United States and finally the Great Depression, touching every corner of the globe. The company did manage a successful response to the downturn, however, noticing that as Americans enjoyed mixing their Bénédictine with brandy, why not do it for them? Within a few years, B&B was outselling bottles of Bénédictine in the U.S. market two to one. This boom carried the Le Grands into the 1970s, when once again they stumbled for lack of aggressive marketing. Fifth-generation Alain was only twenty-nine when the family turned to him for rescue, and little in his résumé of mining, political science, theater, and engineering promised he knew a thing about the booze business. He did, however, bring fresh eyes to his family's situation, rising from marketing director to president by 1981. Martini & Rossi took control of Bénédictine in 1986, with Bacardi buying them out for a reported $1.4 billion six years later.

CHAPTER THREE

THE
BITTERS TRUTH

ANGOSTURA BITTERS

Before we delve into the most famous cocktail ingredient New Orleans ever gave the world—Peychaud's bitters, with deep roots in the Caribbean—let's talk about Angostura, which to this day is produced there. By the 1930s, when Walter Bergeron was trying out his Vieux Carré on drinkers at the Monteleone's Lobby Bar, both bitters had largely left behind thousands of years of production and use for medicinal purpose to find a new and long-lasting home in the world of drinking for pleasure, the world of flavor. As it turns out, from their very beginnings in ancient Egypt, bitters might have been better called bittersweet, since that was the duo of flavor notes they were always intended to bring to anything they touched—and anyone who chose to touch them.

There actually have been archaeological discoveries linking the concept of aromatic bitters to the residue found by chemical analysis inside a wine jar from AD 300–500 in Gebel Adda in southern Egypt. This was hardly the earliest evidence of bitters being used during the Age of the Pharaohs—especially when one realizes that they were considered medicinal remedies for a host of stomach ailments. But identifying what was left of rosemary and pine resin in what had once been sweet Egyptian wine marked the earliest chemical confirmation. "Alcoholic beverages were a good way to get the herbs into solution," offered Patrick McGovern of the University of Pennsylvania in Philadelphia when his 2009 article was published in *Proceedings of the National Academy of Science*. A less technical analysis might be Mary Poppins's: "A spoonful of sugar helps the medicine go down." Throughout history, it seemed with the Egyptian discovery, humans had been infusing the perceived health benefits of nature's many roots, barks, and other botanicals into whatever people could drink with pleasure, or at least without gagging. Thus, bitters were born.

Though the wine jar's evidence might strike the Egypt-savvy as coming a bit late in the saga, that was merely part of the research. Fact is, not one but two jars were analyzed, one from that late date and the other from ca. 3150 BC, found in a tomb in Alydos in upper Egypt that belonged to one of the earliest pharaohs, a leader known as Scorpion I. It was subjected to a twofold analytic process, starting with a test called "liquid chromatography tandem mass spectrometry" to find traces of the tartaric acid that points to wine, then "solid phase microextraction" to find residue from plants. The older jar was found to have the residue of coriander, mint, sage, and pine resin, while the later jar showed only the presence of pine resin. The scientists cautioned that their identification of specific herbs might not be infallible, working with so few of the chemical compounds that were once in the wine. They were less confident of the precise recipe, therefore, than of the idea that such a recipe did exist in ancient Egypt.

The Egyptians may have been the first to seek remedies in the natural world of herbs and other plants, but they were hardly the last. By the Middle Ages, there was even a kind of science grown up around the practice, known then and now as *pharmacognosy*—the study of "physical, chemical, biochemical, and biological properties" of drugs or potential drugs from natural sources. This science, from the Middle Ages and the Renaissance, actually garnered increased interest in the late twentieth and early twenty-first centuries, as many found inspiration in the "holistic" and botany-based medical practices of remote cultures once thought to be primitive. The fact that this inspiration coincided with the craft cocktail movement celebrating old, possibly ancient bitters recipes might or might not have been a coincidence.

Liquids known as "bitters" were a fixture in seventeenth-century England, spreading in popularity to England's colonies in the Americas. This was especially true of sherry-style fortified wines from their namesake, Jerez de la Frontera, as well as from the Canary Islands, Málaga, and Palma de Mallorca. Taken together, these beverages of wine and water infused with botanicals came to be known as "Canary wines." They also helped build a flavor audience for botanicals themselves, which inspired the British to embrace both gin and tonic water, separately and, especially, together. Drinking such things was considered preventive medicine, even long after 1803, when an agricultural magazine called the *Farmer's Cabinet* first used the word "cocktail" without an official definition, and after 1806, when another American publication described a "cocktail" as "a stimulating liquor, composed of spirits of any kind, sugar, water, and bitters."

By this point in history, making bitters had evolved from a solitary, mad-scientist, homebound affair to commercial production. People whipping up said cocktails, whether their motives were medicinal or alcoholic, were buying their bitters from someone. And it wasn't long, for much of the western world, before Angostura became that someone. Although now identified with the Caribbean Island of Trinidad, and fitting in well with its multirace, multiethnic, multi-immigrant flavor profile, the world's best-known brand of "aromatic bitters" wasn't actually created there. A story involving Napoleon Bonaparte, the Prussian section of Germany, still-Spanish Venezuela, Simón Bolívar, and an obviously German doctor named Johann Gottlieb Benjamin Siegert found its fullest expression in a town called Angostura.

In retrospect, Napoleon was the catalyst of the tale, leading his armies of conquest across Europe in the early nineteenth century and, by doing so, inspiring a young medical man to take up arms alongside the Prussians. It was from an army surgeon for the 2nd Regiment that Johann Siegert first learned of enemy Napoleon's concern about stomach upsets affecting the men in his army. According to what we know, Siegert became fascinated with the notion that one can ingest liquids that can indeed settle the stomach, even in the high anxiety of ongoing combat. It was a fascination that stayed with him after Napoleon's final defeat by England's Wellington at Waterloo and exile to St. Helena. Siegert took the idea with him when he heard of Simón Bolívar's revolution against Spain in 1820. Thinking he might be of use, he set sail for Venezuela to join Bolívar in the fight.

The Great Liberator knew promise when he saw it, placing Siegert in charge of the rebel army's hospital, which happened to be situated in the town of Angostura—now known as Ciudad Bolívar—on the banks of the Orinoco River. Before long, the doctor found himself not only treating the wounded in Venezuela's successful struggle for freedom from its colonial overlord but seeking new medicines among the surrounding jungle's bounty of herbs and spices. Four years of seeking pressed him toward a unique, and today highly secret, combination. He named his creation Angostura, after the nearest civilization. In the Spanish spoken all around him, it was an "amargo aromatico," or aromatic bitters.

Due to official gratitude for his years of service to Bolívar, Siegert knew he had a position of comfort and affluence for life with the new Venezuelan republic and its army. But he also knew he had a terrific business idea:

producing his bitters for shipment around the world. In short order, he left the army and chose as his first market segment the closest customers he could find—sailors for all the great colonial powers. They already had come to appreciate Seigert's creation as a treatment for seasickness, and they carried its reputation to other port cities near and far. Business was booming in and around Siegert's facility in Angostura, where the enterprise remained until the doctor's death in 1870. That's when new blood, recognizing a new situation, came up with a new solution.

Siegert's younger brother and three sons took over after his death. And while the family company prospered through a long period of peace in Venezuela, fresh outbreaks of violence in 1875 forced them to rethink their home base. In an act of some desperation, but no small amount of creativity, sons Carlos and Alfredo disguised themselves as British seamen and sneaked aboard a ship bound for Trinidad, one of the more accessible islands. Their brother Luis remained behind to send some production equipment but eventually made it to Trinidad as well. The brothers started fresh on the island, even creating a secret room called The Sanctuary at their production site in Leventile, which was a short distance from Port of Spain. Secrecy, and especially the perception of it, mattered a lot to Carlos, Alfredo, and Luis. To this day, it's said that only five people know the formula for making Angostura bitters. According to the company, the quintet is never allowed to fly on the same airplane or even dine in the same restaurant.

Over the decades, the exotic flavorings and confidential ingredients of Angostura seemed almost to embody the complex population demographics of the once-Spanish island, even though the formula was researched and developed elsewhere in the Spanish colonial world. With a similar population of original Amerindians as other Caribbean islands and, with the coming of Europeans, a similar reliance on African slavery to grow sugar, Trinidad (and its sister island Tobago) took on new, fascinating layerings after the British abolished slavery in 1833. Looking to address a severe labor shortage, as many enslaved people refused the government's "generous offer" of indentured servitude, the British brought in workers from India and later China. These workers found themselves in a suddenly changing environment, as the islands' traditional reliance on growing sugar evolved toward a new reliance on cacao used (primarily in Europe) to make chocolate. Trinidadian cacao became revered around the world, its plantations providing basic livelihoods for some freed slaves as well as for Indians, Chinese, and even Venezuelans experienced in growing cacao back in their own country. The family behind Angostura must have felt strangely at home, surrounded by people who likely had no clue where the town of Angostura actually was.

Still, as things changed in Trinidad and Tobago, things tended not to change around the bitters facility, a place where even mistakes quickly became traditions. In the company's single most celebrated error, the Angostura bottle's oversized label settled in for the duration. The company gives two possible narratives for its creation. One is that one brother was buying the bottles and another buying the labels, and they simply got the measurements wrong. The other story is that the original bottle was lighter in color, clearer, and that the larger label was adopted to protect the bottle from sunlight. Even an eventual change in the bottle size failed to end the tradition, as anyone spotting the label-sheathed container in a retail setting can attest.

Even if resistant to change, Angostura has shown itself open to logical business expansion. Realizing that making bitters is primarily a process of distillation, the company decided to join virtually every other Caribbean island in producing its own rum—a nod to the original sugar by-product that played such a central role in the history of slavery, pirates, empires, and the United States. Angostura was already making its own wooden barrels for aging bitters and running its own school for "cooperage." Organized by a veteran of the Scotch industry, the school program provides training not only for Angostura employees but for those sent by rum producers on other islands. Recent trainees have traveled to Trinidad from Jamaica and St. Lucia. The goal, according to the company, is to keep a necessary and traditional trade alive.

Dr. Siegert's three sons ran the company into the twentieth century, with the first, Carlos, passing away in 1903.

That very year Alfredo was appointed purveyor of bitters to the king of Prussia (surely his father would have been proud) and in 1907 to the king of Spain. Two years later, despite the Spanish-accented name, J. G. B. Siegert & Hijos became a public limited liability company registered in England. Though Angostura's rum production had roots in the early 1900s, things got serious in 1936 when one Robert Siegert, a trained chemist who was a great-grandson of the founder, joined the company. The spirit would play a large role in acquisition attractiveness, inspiring CL Financial to buy 78 percent of Angostura in 1997 and to found CL World brand in 2003. In 2017 Genevieve Jodhan made history being appointed Angostura's first female CEO.

As we know, Dr. Siegert created the original Angostura formula from jungle herbs to calm men's stomachs before battle and to help sailors recover from seasickness—both essentially medicinal uses that even the Egyptian pharaohs would understand. Still, Angostura found its true destiny in mixology, its long journey capped dramatically by its 2001 decision to launch the Global Cocktail Challenge. Over the years, as many as a thousand bartenders have competed in the event, a group eventually narrowed down to twelve and finally to three. In 2020, the winning mixologist hailed from the Bahamas, while second place went to a bartender from Tasmania and third to one from Vietnam. The winning entry, called Mas Curried, captures one of the most iconic "Trini" flavors—Indian curry—combines it with cauliflower, weaves in the company's orange bitters, and manages to showcase Angostura 7 Year Old Rum, with what its makers describe as "rich maple, chocolate, honey and toffee notes."

As one of the judges was heard to understate at the time: "His rum cocktail was probably the most unusual of the competition. I'd never considered adding cauliflower to a cocktail, but it really works." When the Trinidadians of Angostura say "global," they really do mean global.

PEYCHAUD'S BITTERS

Antoine Amédée Peychaud has got to be the godfather, or at least the poster child, of the New Orleans cocktail. For one thing, the cocktail bitters he created and served in his apothecary shop on Royal Street still figures mightily in the first New Orleans cocktail to get a name and a recipe, even though that recipe has evolved over time: the Sazerac. For another, Peychaud was credited for much of the twentieth century with inventing the word "cocktail" itself. We know he served alcoholic toddies in a so-called "egg cup" (*coquetier* in French) that then, according to the popular story, was Americanized by non–French-speakers into "cock-tay" and finally "cocktail." It was a sad day in New Orleans when we realized the word cocktail was actually already in use by the time Peychaud started working his bitter magic, whether as medicine or as drinking pleasure. For many years, apparently, the frontier between the two was pretty murky.

The fact is, one of Peychaud's greatest—though often unmentioned—claims to fame was hailing from the one place on earth that had the most to say about the flavors, smells, rhythms, and cultures of New Orleans, the Caribbean island of Saint-Domingue. We know it today, of course, as Haiti.

A French colony up until and slightly beyond the French Revolution of 1789, Saint-Domingue was ground zero of the Caribbean sugar trade. It was also home to a bustling trade in coffee, which would figure into Peychaud's sometimes ambiguous origin story, the one concerning whether he was actually born on the island or in New Orleans. It was on Saint-Domingue, and certain other islands, that sugar turned ambitious young entrepreneurs with little to recommend them into sugar plantation barons. Generations grew rich off the sweet stuff, which was wildly desirable from New York to London and Paris. They also became intoxicated from sugar's byproduct, molasses, once it had been distilled into rum. All of this wealth came to depend on free labor on Saint-Domingue, as it did in Louisiana and other southern states that set themselves up along Caribbean lines. Growing sugar was labor intensive, which was another way of saying the population of Saint-Domingue worked and grew and prospered its way into becoming a small, French-speaking white minority and a large, often illiterate, and constantly abused majority of Black enslaved people from Africa. That's who revolted violently against their French colonial overlords between 1791 and 1804, slaughtering many and sending even more climbing aboard any ship they could find to port cities like New Orleans. The Peychauds were, by the time of the Haitian Revolution, among the refugees.

In recent years, a new generation of historians has pondered deeply the questions raised by this slave insurrection, knowing full well that Haiti's troubles during the twentieth century as the poorest nation in the Western Hemisphere would convince some that the place was of marginal importance. Far from it, say these historians. The bloody overthrow of a white minority by a Black majority stirred profound interest at the sugar plantations along the Mississippi upriver from New Orleans, where a revolt did indeed break out a few years later in 1811, inspired by Haiti's revolution. The enslaved people who marched to New Orleans to found their own Black republic were captured, tortured, and executed, many of their heads displayed on pikes along the river levees as a warning. With even greater lasting and tragic impact on America, white minorities across the slave states (and elsewhere) sought to unite the surrounding ragtag, usually brawling mix of French, Spanish, Italian, Irish, German, Greek, Croatian, and other immigrants into a body that could survive the Black "menace." They came to call themselves something they hadn't exactly thought of before. They referred to themselves as "white."

It was into this charged climate that the Peychaud family relocated in the first years of the nineteenth century. They had, after all, done great, ambitious things in the past, going back to the matchless southwest French wine region Bordeaux. There is still a respected French Bordeaux made by Chateau Peychaud. There, along the Gironde River, ambitious families started building wine dynasties. And since the actual classification of Bordeaux estates didn't take place until much later, 1855, families could be whatever they claimed to be. They often did business with increasing numbers of British middlemen, who insisted upon calling the local product by the ridiculously un-French name "claret." Barrel after barrel of the great-tasting stuff found its way into cellars and onto tables on the far side of the English Channel. Still, for Antoine's grandparents, the

New World was a magnet that could not be resisted. And it wasn't sugar that attracted them. It was coffee.

It would seem, from the dates we know, that the Peychauds had little time to establish themselves as a force in Saint-Domingue. Coffee, of course, was already a major export product, grown on the hillsides and mountainsides, the higher the altitude the better. It was a tough, competitive business, one that took it on the chin from Mother Nature at regular intervals. It could be too hot or too cold, too wet or too dry, and sometimes a hurricane (long before such storms were given human names) tore through and destroyed the labor of a year, a decade, or a lifetime. Arguably, coffee was the original desired crop in Saint-Domingue, since the first French explorer to the island had brought live coffee plants in his quarters, keeping them alive through a becalming at sea by sharing his own water ration. That explorer, one Gabriel de Clieu by name, was the father of the Haitian coffee industry, with cuttings from his plants making it to many other Caribbean islands and throughout the New World.

We don't know how or why the Peychauds avoided building a sugar plantation, since the return on investment seemed several times greater than that of coffee. They probably did use enslaved people to grow and pick the green coffee beans, though the job could be handled by far fewer than the armies required for the cultivation and the dangerous processing of sugar. Coffee beans would have received only a light bit of processing, then be bagged as green coffee and delivered to the dock for shipment. Some of it, no doubt, was taken to Paris, creating a demand that, as its producers understood it, only more coffee could meet. Much of the product, though, went to New Orleans, where a coffee-drinking culture was born that rivaled that of its forebears in Paris, London, Vienna, and Venice. It's enticing to think that Antoine Amédée Peychaud grew to manhood in New Orleans surrounded by a family that understood fine wine from Bordeaux and great coffee from Haiti.

As a port city accustomed to and dependent upon immigration, New Orleans already had inklings of what a difference an arriving culture can make. A French city since its founding, New Orleans had seen nothing less iconic than its original French Quarter destroyed twice by fire and rebuilt during a brief period of Spanish control. Thus, the part of the city meant to mirror France ended up looking less like Paris than like Old San Juan. Despite this awareness, however, New Orleans would never, before or since the Haitian Revolution, experience its population almost doubling with refugees from a single place. Not quite yet a state in the Union, Louisiana in and around New Orleans would grow overnight with a Creole patois–speaking population—Black, white, and most tones in between—that craved spicy food, outfits formed of wildly colorful fabrics, and dancing—not to violins and harpsichords but drums. Nearly everything visitors associate with New Orleans to this day arrived on ships fleeing what had to be some of human history's bloodiest slave revolts.

In recent years, with the renaissance of craft cocktails, many of which make use of Peychaud's namesake bitters, the incorrect story about how the man invented the cocktail has been replaced by a real curiosity about what he did and how he did it, starting with when and where he was born. Establishing the year of his birth, 1803, didn't quite settle things, since that could have fallen either in Haiti or in New Orleans after the Peychauds had escaped. Still, evidence has slowly gathered around what had been the original story, told by at least two chroniclers of the apothecary's life.

"One refugee succeeded in salvaging, among other scanty possessions, a recipe for the compounding of a liquid tonic, called *bitters*, a recipe that had been a secret family formula for years," wrote Stanley Clisby Arthur in 1937. "This particular young Creole refugee was of a distinguished French family and had been educated as an apothecary. His name was Antoine Amédée Peychaud. In the turmoil of the insurrection and the hurried exodus from San Domingo, Amédée and his younger sister became separated." While not revered for faithfulness to fact, Arthur does seem to be building his narrative on the earlier work of an actual New Orleans historian, Grace King. In her 1921 book *Creole Families of New Orleans*, King says of Antoine: "He and his sister, Lasthénie, were saved from massacre in the insurrection of the slaves by their nurse, but in the panic of the moment the children became separated and the boy was brought to New Orleans alone."

Building on the work of King, Arthur, and others, much later historians have established that Charles Peychaud from Bordeaux became a wealthy coffee planter on the northern part of the island, an area now known as Cap-Haitian. His son, also named Charles, became a physician. He and his wife had two children while still on Saint-Domingue, Lasthénie around 1799 and Antoine in 1803, only one year before the island became an independent nation. With this information, we are safe saying that the Peychaud family was among the last to escape for New Orleans.

It was tempting for decades to imagine Antoine training as an apothecary and even creating the formula for his bitters while still living in Haiti, thus lending a bit of voodoo to the formulation. But unless he completed his studies and his experiments at age one or two, this clearly didn't happen. The lad grew up in New Orleans, drawing from his family and the city around him a curiosity about medicines marked at that time by the guiding presence of alcohol. Whoever really invented the name cocktail, it didn't enter Antoine's vocabulary as the drink it came to be but as the consumable guarantor of good health and longevity. By 1841, Antoine Peychaud had set up his Pharmacie Peychaud on Royal Street and begun dispensing a patented aniseed and gentian herbal remedy that he called Peychaud's Bitters. At the pharmacy, however, he not only sold his bitters by the bottle but by the cup—a rudimentary toddy made by mixing the bitters with water, sugar, and French brandy. It was the pharmacist's prescription for practically any ailment.

From 1841 until his death in 1880, Antoine Peychaud built his business with insight and energy. He also showed, for his day, a remarkable sensitivity to changes in the city he had loved since it took him and his family in out of the Haitian storm. After all, 1803 wasn't merely the year of Antoine's birth; it was also the year Thomas Jefferson agreed to pay French emperor Napoleon $15 million for the vast territory stretching from the Gulf of Mexico to Canada, known then as Louisiana. In the years since, French Louisi-

Newspaper ad for Peychaud's bitters.

ana had become an American state, and its long-dominant Creole families had lost prestige to the "American" families that sought to make the other side of Canal Street (including the Garden District) the rival of the French Quarter in every way. Though he belonged to a Creole family with deeper roots than most—going back to colonial Saint-Domingue, no less—and surely served many an old Creole a toddy in his pharmacy, Peychaud showed little interest in fighting such tired, meaningless battles. He seemed to welcome the open doors that belonging to the United States brought to his commerce.

Peychaud's life was one of slow, careful redefinition, from a pharmacist who behaved more like a barkeep to a manufacturer of an iconic product that soon found a market across the state, then the nation, and eventually the world. His bitters found its first high-profile home in the recipe for the Sazerac, joining the cognac made by Sazerac de Forge et Fils that gave the drink its name. This became the recipe at the Merchants Exchange, also known as the Merchants Coffee House, in the French Quarter. By the time the place changed its name to the Sazerac Coffee House around 1852, it had a bar that was 125 feet long and that was tended by no fewer than a dozen bartenders making almost nothing else.

The growth of the Sazerac as the original cocktail of New Orleans would carry Peychaud's bitters out to the world along with it. By 1870 Peychaud would close his apothecary shop to enter into business with a decidedly non-Creole named Thomas Handy, who had once helped operate the Sazerac Coffee House. Their company became the sole importer of Sazerac brandy and the manufacturer of Peychaud's bitters. By the time of his death ten years later, Antoine Amédée Peychaud and his business partner had a virtual monopoly on the city's most popular drink. And by then, just about anybody speaking just about any language would call the Sazerac a cocktail.

In recent years, the Peychaud name has entered a few arenas its creator surely never envisioned. Now controlled by the Sazerac Company, an entity known for aggressively protecting its trademarks as well as promoting them, Peychaud has become even more of a household word among both tourists and locals in New Orleans. For one thing, while the bulk of each year's bitters production now comes from Sazerac's Buffalo Trace Distillery in Kentucky, a measurable amount is distilled right in the Crescent City. The new Sazerac House on Canal Street is part museum of the iconic cocktail and part (even if a small part) bitters factory, letting people watch the entire process much as they might at an ice cream or sauce company offering tours. Since the bitters were served in the original Sazerac at the original

Peychaud's bottling line. Courtesy Sazerac Company.

Sazerac House in the 1850s, the whole business seems logical enough. At the conclusion of their visit, fans can even purchase bottles of Peychaud's bitters made on site.

And then, this being the twenty-first century, there's licensing. The Sazerac Company is no newcomer to the concept, having licensed its name for many years to the legendary Sazerac Bar at the Roosevelt Hotel. Bartenders there spend much of every day turning out first-rate Sazeracs, though still other customers wander in to visit the striking Paul Ninas murals of New Orleans life, painted during his stint as a WPA artist in the 1930s. In 2021, as the world struggled to recover from the Covid-19 pandemic, local cocktail man Neal Bodenheimer opened a small bar just off the courtyard of the tiny-but-chic Hotel Maison de Ville. The bar's name should not be a surprise to anyone familiar with local cocktail history, or at least with the Sazerac Company's love of licensing. Serving Sazeracs and Vieux Carrés, along with other New Orleans favorites like the Ojen cocktail and the bubbly French 75, the new watering hole is called Peychaud's.

"For me, that connection was enough to want to do this," Bodenheimer told one news reporter. "I consider Peychaud the most important figure in New Orleans cocktails. His product is in everything."

CHAPTER FOUR

RECIPES

The "problem" of every great cocktail is balance, and every recipe and every bartender solves the problem a little bit differently. Still, both before and just after Prohibition, most worthy drink recipes avoided the less-admirable solutions we taste so often today. The drinks then were generally "booze-forward," sidestepping the heavy hand of cheap citrus and sugar that many classicists now decry. Especially when seated at a bar or table in New Orleans, none of the booze-forward drinks of the era is likely to taste better than our chosen cocktail.

VIEUX CARRÉ

Drinkers of the analytical sort have noted the impressive balance of flavors in the original Vieux Carré recipe created at the Monteleone by Walter Bergeron. Still, at its heart, the drink is a balancing act among the sweet, the not-so-sweet, and the bitterly botanical. Most drink recipes, of course, would call for one of arguably the two best-known brands of bitters. The Vieux Carré calls for both. As with cooking a dish for dinner at home, there is always some wiggle room to account for personal taste. Here is the classic recipe.

1 ounce rye whiskey

1 ounce cognac

1 ounce sweet vermouth

¼ ounce Bénédictine

2 dashes Peychaud's bitters

2 dashes Angostura bitters

Lemon peel for garnish

Add all the ingredients to a mixing glass, add ice cubes, and stir. Strain the cocktail into a rocks glass with fresh ice. Garnish with a lemon peel.

THE MODERN VIEUX CARRÉ

This modern tropical spin on the Vieux Carré is officially called the Vieux Ananas, and its creation using the Plantation Pineapple Rum instead of cognac is appropriate to New Orleans in all kinds of ways. For more than a century, New Orleans was the single most important port of entry for pineapples (*ananas* in several languages), bananas, and other tropical fruits from the Caribbean and Central America. "Pineapple rum is so good in stirred drinks," says bartender Ezra Star of Drink in Boston. "The body and weight of the Barbados distillate gives this flavor you don't expect to be there with pineapple, but because of it you can use it almost like a brandy." Other bartenders have come up with intriguing variations: Banana liqueur and two types of cardamom enhance Anthony Auger's Vieux Carré at Benne on Eagle in Asheville, North Carolina. And in the Carried Away from Matthew Grippo of Blackbird in San Francisco, a rye bread–infused cognac is supported by Bonal, sweet vermouth, Bénédictine, bitters, and a rinse of absinthe infused with pu-erh tea.

1 ounce rye whiskey

1 ounce Plantation
   Pineapple Rum

1 ounce sweet vermouth

½ ounce Bénédictine

1 dash Angostura bitters

Orange twist for garnish

Stir ingredients together in a mixing glass with ice. Strain over a large ice cube into a double Old Fashioned glass.

NEGRONI

We might call the Negroni an Italian Vieux Carré, though since the Negroni is older, we probably ought to call the Vieux Carré a New Orleans Negroni. Either way, the classic is, if anything, equally complicated and satisfying in its flavor profile. It's both sweet and bitter, of course—but also dry and refreshing thanks to one of its few ingredients being gin. As once was observed, the Negroni ingredient list is proof that good things come in threes, "like Stooges and Musketeers." The Negroni was, according to the most-accepted legend, invented for a Count Negroni by his favorite bartender, Forsco Scarselli, at Café Casoni in Florence in 1919. It was a fresh spin on the count's longtime favorite, the Americano. The drink became one of the most popular aperitifs in northern Italy throughout the twentieth century, being embraced by the craft cocktail movement late in the century. One much-enjoyed variation, especially in the summer, is the Negroni Spagliato, made with the Italian sparkling wine called spumante instead of gin. The name means a "Messed-Up Negroni," since the drink's invention was allegedly an accident by a too-busy bartender.

1 ounce dry gin

1 ounce Campari

1 ounce sweet vermouth

Orange peel for garnish

Mix the ingredients with ice in a shaker and stir. Strain into a rocks glass over ice. Garnish with orange peel. Note: some current bartenders even break with Negroni tradition and shake the shaker lightly to give it a light froth.

LA LOUISIANE COCKTAIL

It's pretty hard to ignore a drink often called "the secret cocktail of New Orleans," even though the same could have been said of the Vieux Carré before its reemergence in the twenty-first century. Some believe the La Louisiane shows the influence of the Monteleone's signature cocktail, setting its creation in stone no earlier than the late 1930s. Others insist that, no, it was probably created much earlier, at a French Quarter restaurant called La Louisiane, first opened by the family behind Antoine's in the 1880s. The ingredients are quite similar, as is the alcoholic intent. As La Louisiane restaurant closed some years back after a parade of different owners, the La Louisiane cocktail is now most often found at the bar of the posh Windsor Court Hotel. Still, one of its most high-visibility appearances was at the closing sessions of the Tales of the Cocktail conference in 2015, thanks to mixologists from the local bar Cure. In recent years, with the connected nature of bartenders around the world, the La Louisiane has made it onto menus in New York City, San Francisco, and even Sydney, Australia.

2 ounces rye whiskey

¾ ounce sweet vermouth

½ ounce Bénédictine

3 dashes absinthe

3 dashes Peychaud's bitters

Maraschino cherry for garnish

Add the rye whiskey, sweet vermouth, Bénédictine, absinthe, and Peychaud's bitters into a mixing glass with ice and stir until well chilled. Strain into a chilled coupe glass. Garnish with a skewered maraschino cherry.

THE MARTINEZ

If we are to believe what many cocktail historians tell us, the drink with the popular Hispanic surname has quite a claim to fame. Though its origins remain unclear, and there's even a California city named Martinez that claims its invention, most agree it played a role in the recipe and name of a far more iconic cocktail, the martini. Cocktail legend Jerry Thomas may have invented the drink for someone traveling to the port city of that name, since the concept made its earliest-known appearance in print in the 1884 book *The Modern Bartender's Guide,* by O. H. Byron. Interestingly, English gin had not yet risen to the top of the heap in America, a place where the Dutch *genever* still reigned. This malty-style gin probably shone at the heart of this recipe, though of course the English gin of your choice also works fine. The Martinez became forever associated with Thomas in 1887, when a posthumous edition of his *The Bar-Tender's Guide* appeared. His recipe called for Old Tom gin, which fell dead center between the malty Dutch *genever* and the juniper-heavy London dry style. It's convincing that the Martinez continued to evolve, moving more and more toward the dry martini loved by James Bond and millions of others today.

1½ ounces gin

1½ ounces sweet vermouth

¼ ounce Luxardo
   maraschino liqueur

2 dashes Angostura bitters

Orange twist for garnish

Add the gin, sweet vermouth, maraschino liqueur, and bitters into a mixing glass with ice and stir until well chilled. Strain into a chilled coupe glass. Garnish with an orange twist.

THE BRANDY CRUSTA

Sicilians and other Italians played a major role in New Orleans cocktail history, even beyond Antonio Monteleone giving the Vieux Carré cocktail and Walter Bergeron himself a near-permanent home. A bartender named Joseph Santini created the Brandy Crusta in the 1850s at his French Quarter bar called Jewel of the South, and following the taste of his era, his recipe tended to be tart. Forgotten for decades, the Brandy Crusta appeared ready for its new closeup in 2004, when Chris Hannah of Arnaud's French 75 adjusted Santini's recipe a bit sweeter for modern taste preferences. Tart or sweet, the key to a well-made Crusta remains a perfect balance between the two. The drink is considered one of the original and inspirational cocktail sours. Among its flavor progeny is the Sidecar.

Sugar for rim

2 ounces cognac or other brandy

¼ ounce curaçao

½ ounce fresh lemon juice

½ ounce simple syrup

1 teaspoon maraschino liqueur

1 dash Angostura bitters

Lemon twist for garnish

Rim a coupe glass with sugar. Add all ingredients into a shaker with ice and shake. Strain into the prepared glass. Garnish with a lemon twist.

THE ROB ROY

One of the clear inspirations for the Vieux Carré, the traditional Manhattan made its debut in the city it names in about 1880. Within just over a decade, bartenders at the original Waldorf Astoria Hotel were leaving out the rye and pouring in Scotch whisky instead. Unless you're a dyed-in-the-wool Scotch drinker, the notion might seem strange, but lovers of the Rob Roy insist on ordering it every chance they get. Frank Caiafa, New York bartender and author of *The Waldorf Astoria Bar Book*, says the drink was inspired by an operetta performed at the nearby Herald Square Theatre. The product from Scotland is standing in for Rob Roy MacGregor, a Robin Hood–like hero of both the operetta and Scottish folklore. Most today would say the key is letting the Scotch speak for itself—in other words, not covering its taste with too much sweet vermouth and bitters. Still, many prefer the more subtle flavors of blended Scotch to the uber-peaty taste of your favorite single malt.

2 ounces scotch

¾ ounce sweet vermouth

3 dashes Angostura bitters

2 brandied cherries for garnish

Add the scotch, sweet vermouth, and bitters into a mixing glass with ice and stir until well chilled. Strain into a chilled cocktail glass. Garnish with 2 speared brandied cherries.

SOURCES

Adams, Jenny. *Hotel Monteleone: More Than a Landmark, the Heart of New Orleans since 1886.* Virginia Beach: Donnin Company, 2011.

Baird, Sarah. *New Orleans Cocktails: An Elegant Collection of Over 100 Recipes Inspired by the Big Easy.* New York: Cider Mill Press, 2017.

Bannos, Jimmy, and John DeMers. *Big Easy Cocktails: Jazzy Drinks and Savory Bites from New Orleans.* Berkeley: Ten Speed Press, 2006.

Charming, Cheryl. *The Cocktail Companion: A Guide to Cocktail History, Culture, Trivia and Favorite Drinks.* Coral Gables: Mango Publishing, 2018.

DeGroff, Dale. *The Craft of the Cocktail: Everything You Need to Know to Be a Master Bartender, with 500 Recipes.* New York: Clarkson Potter, 2002.

Felten, Eric. *How's Your Drink? Cocktails, Culture, and the Art of Drinking Well.* Chicago: Agate Surrey Books, 2007.

Ford, Adam. *Vermouth: The Revival of the Spirit That Created America's Cocktail Culture.* Woodstock: The Countryman Press, 2015.

Hess, Robert B. "Peychaud Bitters." Drinkboy's Weblog. Small Screen Network. Archived from the video podcast, June 13, 2008, and Sept. 29, 2017.

Jarrard, Kyle. *Cognac: The Seductive Saga of the World's Most Coveted Spirit.* Hoboken: John Wiley & Sons, 2005.

Larson, Susan, Alexandra Collier, and Phillip Collier. *New Orleans' Literary Landmark: Hotel Monteleone.* New Orleans: Hotel Monteleone, 2015.

McNally, Tim. *The Sazerac.* Baton Rouge: Louisiana State University Press, 2020.

Meyer, Mark, and Meredith Meyer Grelli. *The Whiskey Rebellion and the Rebirth of Rye: A Pittsburgh Story.* Cleveland: Belt Publishing, 2017.

Sazerac Company website. www.sazerachouse.com and www.sazerac.com.

Williams, Elizabeth M., and Chris McMillian. *Lift Your Spirits: A Celebratory History of Cocktail Culture in New Orleans.* Baton Rouge: Louisiana State University Press, 2016.

Wondrich, David. *Imbibe! From Absinthe Cocktail to Whiskey Smash: A Salute in Stories and Drinks to "Professor" Jerry Thomas, Pioneer of the American Bar.* Updated and revised ed. New York: TarcherPerigee, 2015.

ICONIC NEW ORLEANS COCKTAILS

The Sazerac

The Café Brûlot

The Vieux Carré

The Absinthe Frappé